Have you stepped on a pin lately? Can't find a pin when you need one? You need more pincushions! With this cute collection of fifteen easy-to-sew pincushions, you'll have one for every room in the house.

Beginners can master the simple Stacked pincushion and the ribbon-enhanced Trio, which features three ways to decorate a simple square with ribbon. The Log Cabin and Tufted designs are favorites in modern prints. More experienced sewers will delight in making the Pleated and flower-like Prairie Points pincushions. Everyone can practice their embroidery skills with Layered Squares.

These mixed-fabric designs allow you to use small amounts of fabric in vibrant modern colors. Choose prints to match your personality and decor and add ribbons and other embellishments for a whimsical touch. Let your personality shine while you whip out a dozen or so pincushions for yourself and all your friends.

LEISURE ARTS, INC. • Maumelle, Arkansas

wrist

SHOPPING LIST

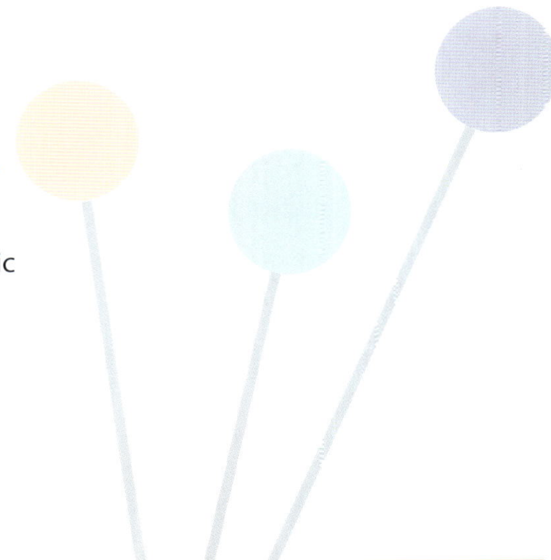

- ☐ $2\frac{1}{2}$" x $4\frac{1}{2}$" rectangle of polka dot print cotton fabric
- ☐ $2\frac{1}{2}$" x $4\frac{1}{2}$" rectangle and 2" x $9\frac{1}{2}$" strip of floral print cotton fabric
- ☐ $5\frac{1}{2}$" length of $\frac{1}{2}$" wide elastic
- ☐ three $\frac{1}{2}$" diameter felt ball embellishments
- ☐ all-purpose sewing thread
- ☐ safety pin
- ☐ polyester fiberfill

*Please read **Basics**, page 31, before beginning project.*

To make the Pincushion

***Note:** Match right sides and raw edges and use a $\frac{1}{4}$" seam allowance throughout. Press seam allowances open after sewing each seam.*

1. Matching long edges, fold strip in half. Sew long raw edges together to make a tube.
2. Attach safety pin to 1 end of tube. Pushing pin through tube, turn tube right side out. Centering seam, press tube flat.
3. Attach safety pin to 1 end of elastic length. Use pin to thread elastic through tube. Before you pull the elastic length all the way through, pin the opposite end to the end of the tube. Fabric will gather onto elastic.
4. Pin remaining end of elastic even with end of tube. To secure the elastic, sew across ends of tube with a narrow seam.
5. With seam facing up, baste ends of tube to center of each short edge of polka dot rectangle.
6. With tube sandwiched in between, sew polka dot rectangle and floral print rectangle together, leaving about $1\frac{1}{2}$" open on 1 long edge for turning. Trim seam allowances at corners.
7. Turn pincushion right side out; press. Press seam allowances at opening $\frac{1}{4}$" to inside.
8. Fill pincushion with fiberfill. Whipstitch the opening closed.
9. Hand sew the balls to 1 corner of the pincushion top.

round

SHOPPING LIST

- ☐ 2 1/2" x 17" strip of floral print cotton fabric for sides
- ☐ 5" x 5" square of pink print cotton fabric for bottom
- ☐ 5" x 5" square of orange print cotton fabric for top
- ☐ 1 yard of 1/4" wide decorative braid
- ☐ all-purpose sewing thread
- ☐ fabric glue
- ☐ tracing paper
- ☐ filling of choice (see page 31)

*Please read **Basics**, page 31, before beginning project.*

To make the Pincushion

***Note:** Match right sides and raw edges and use a 1/4" seam allowance throughout.*

1. Trace pattern onto tracing paper, ignoring long lines along edge. Using pattern, cut 1 circle from each square.

2. Press 1 short end of floral print strip 1/4" to wrong side.

3. Referring to **Fig. 1**, begin with the pressed end and pin the sides to the top around the edge of the circle; ends will overlap. Baste along edge, stopping 1/2" from beginning of basting. Leaving a 1" overlap, trim excess fabric. Press remaining end of sides 1/4" to wrong side and complete basting **(Fig. 2)**.

4. Stitching along basting line, sew top to sides; clip seam allowances.

5. Baste bottom to sides, overlapping ends as above.

6. Stitching along basting line, sew bottom to sides; clip seam allowances.

7. Turn pincushion right side out; press.

8. Fill pincushion with your choice of filling. Whipstitch the opening closed.

9. Trimming ends to fit as needed, glue braid around top and bottom seams.

Fig. 1

Fig. 2

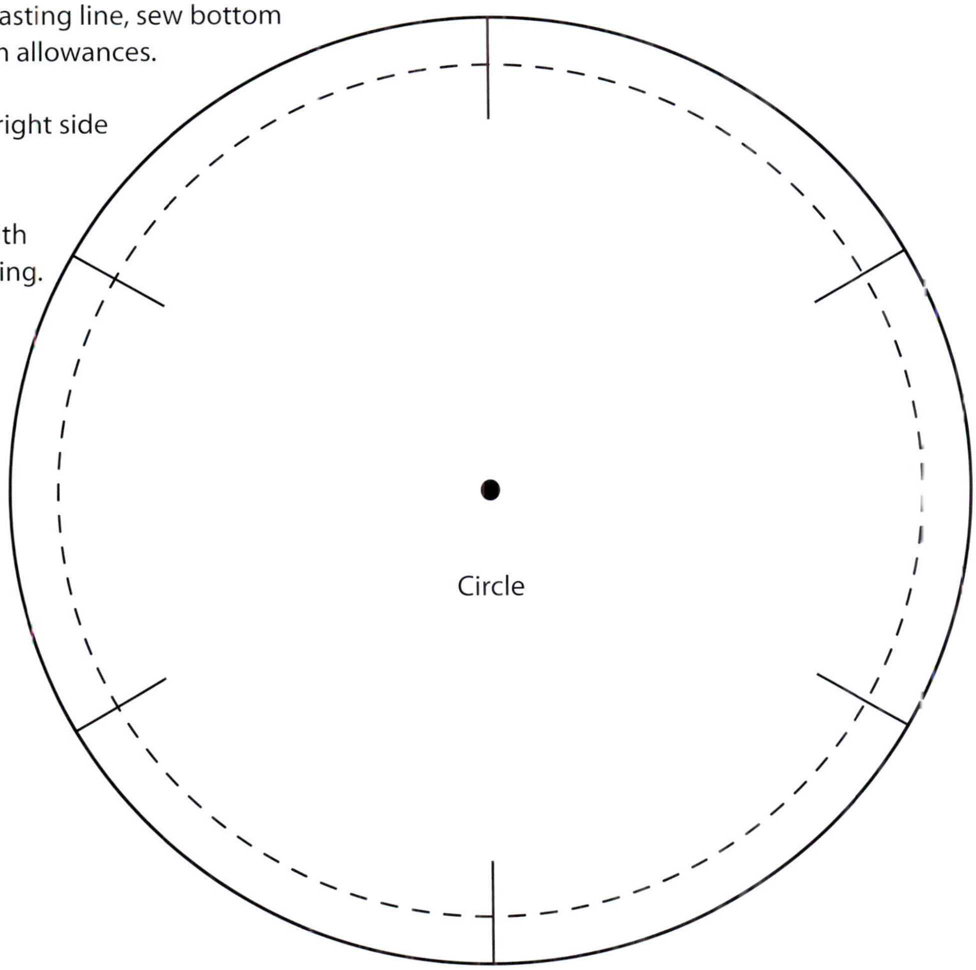

tufted

SHOPPING LIST

- ☐ two 5" x 5" squares of purple cotton fabric
- ☐ lavender size #5 pearl cotton
- ☐ all-purpose sewing thread
- ☐ 3/4" diameter decorative button
- ☐ 3/4" diameter purple button
- ☐ embroidery needle
- ☐ air- or water-soluble fabric marking pen
- ☐ tracing paper
- ☐ filling of choice (see page 31)

*Please read **Basics**, page 31, before beginning project.*

To make the Pincushion

***Note:** Use pattern, page 5. Match right sides and raw edges and use a 1/4" seam allowance throughout.*

1. Trace pattern onto tracing paper. Using pattern, cut 2 circles from fabric.

2. Using marking pen, place a small dot in the center of each circle on the right side of the fabric. Place marks as indicated on pattern on the right side of the fabric around the outside edge of each circle.

3. Aligning marks, sew circles together, leaving about 1 1/2" open for turning. Clip seam allowances.

4. Turn pincushion right side out; press. Press seam allowances at opening 1/4" to inside.

5. Fill pincushion with your choice of filling. Whipstitch the opening closed.

6. To determine length needed, wrap the pearl cotton top to bottom around the pincushion 8 times. Measure this length and multiply by 2. Cut pearl cotton to this length.

7. Thread needle and knot the ends together to form a doubled strand. Take a few stitches on the bottom center of the pincushion to secure the pearl cotton. Bring the needle straight up through the center of the pincushion from bottom to top.

8. Bring pearl cotton around outside edge of pincushion at 1 of the marks on the edge and insert the needle again from bottom to top through center. Tug gently to seat the pearl cotton into the pincushion to create a tufted effect. Moving the pearl cotton around to the next mark, repeat at each mark to make a total of 6 tufted sections.

9. Insert needle under 1 of the section dividers **(Fig. 1)** and pull tautly. Insert the needle under the opposite section divider and pull tautly. Insert needle from top to bottom through center, then again from bottom to top through center to secure. Do **not** cut pearl cotton.

10. Place decorative button on top of pincushion and remaining button on bottom. Working through center, stitch both buttons on at the same time. Secure pearl cotton with a few stitches under the bottom button; trim pearl cotton.

Fig. 1

pyramid

SHOPPING LIST

- ☐ five 5" x 5" squares of coordinating cotton fabrics
- ☐ 1 yd of baby rickrack
- ☐ all-purpose sewing thread
- ☐ fabric glue
- ☐ tracing paper
- ☐ filling of choice (see page 31)

Please read ***Basics****, page 31, before beginning project.*

To make the Pincushion

Note: *Match right sides and raw edges and use a 1/4" seam allowance throughout.*

1. Trace pattern onto tracing paper. Using pattern, cut 4 triangles. Cut 1 square 3 3/4" x 3 3/4".
2. Using pattern, sew 2 triangles together along 1 angled side from the bottom to the top, stopping at top dot; backstitch. Trim seam allowances above dot. Press seam allowances open. Repeat with 2 remaining triangles.
3. Keeping seam allowances open, sew triangle pairs together along remaining sides from the bottom to the top, stopping at top dot; backstitch. Trim seam allowances above dot. Press seam allowances open.
4. Pivoting at dots, sew square to bottom edges of triangles, leaving about 1 1/2" open for turning. Trim seam allowances at corners.
5. Turn pincushion right side out; press. Press seam allowances at opening 1/4" to inside.
6. Fill pincushion with your choice of filling. Whipstitch the opening closed.
7. Cut 2 7" lengths of rickrack. Glue 1 length from side to side along seamlines across top of pincushion. Repeat with remaining length along remaining top seamlines. Trim ends as needed.
8. Cut a 14" length of rickrack. Glue length along bottom seamline of pincushion. Trim ends as needed.

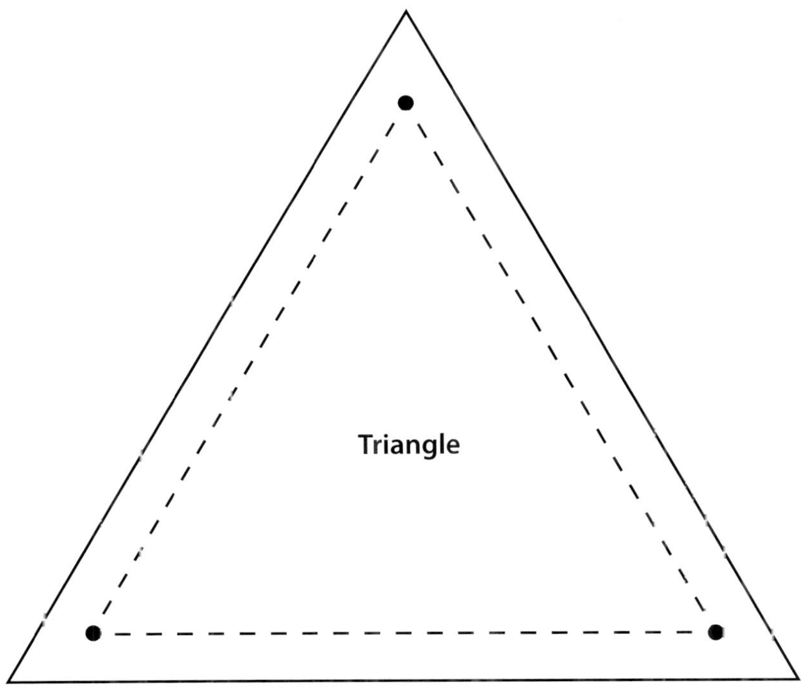

log cabin

SHOPPING LIST

- ☐ $1^1/_2$" x $1^1/_2$" square (A) and $2^1/_2$" x $5^1/_2$" rectangle (F) of brown print cotton fabric
- ☐ $1^1/_2$" x $1^1/_2$" square (A), $1^1/_2$" x $2^1/_2$" rectangle (B), and $2^1/_2$" x $5^1/_2$" rectangle (F) of green print cotton fabric
- ☐ $1^1/_2$" x $2^1/_2$" rectangle (B), $1^1/_2$" x $3^1/_2$" rectangle (C), and $2^1/_2$" x $5^1/_2$" rectangle (F) of turquoise print cotton fabric
- ☐ $1^1/_2$" x $3^1/_2$" rectangle (C) and $1^1/_2$" x $4^1/_2$" rectangle (D) of floral print cotton fabric
- ☐ $1^1/_2$" x $4^1/_2$" rectangle (D) and $1^1/_2$" x $5^1/_2$" rectangle (E) of orange print cotton fabric
- ☐ all-purpose sewing thread
- ☐ fabric glue
- ☐ filling of choice (see page 31)

*Please read **Basics**, page 31, before beginning project.*

To make the Pincushion

***Note:** Match right sides and raw edges and use a 1/4" seam allowance throughout. Press seam allowances open after sewing each seam.*

1. To make pincushion top, refer to **Fig. 1** and work from the center out to sew squares and rectangles together.
2. To make pincushion bottom, refer to **Fig. 2**, to sew rectangles F together.
3. Sew top and bottom together, leaving about 1 1/2" open for turning. Trim seam allowances at corners.
4. Turn pincushion right side out; press. Press seam allowances at opening 1/4" to inside.
5. Fill cushion with your choice of filling. Whipstitch the opening closed.

Fig. 1

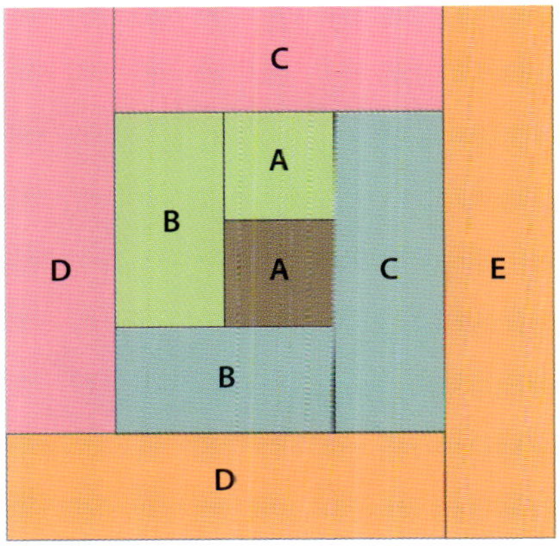

Fig. 2

cube

SHOPPING LIST

- ☐ six 4" x 4" squares of assorted coordinating print cotton fabrics
- ☐ 1 1/2 yards of 1/4" wide decorative braid
- ☐ all-purpose sewing thread
- ☐ fabric glue
- ☐ filling of choice (see page 31)

*Please read **Basics**, page 31, before beginning project.*

To make the Pincushion

***Note:** Match right sides and raw edges and use a 1/4" seam allowance throughout. Begin and end stitching lines exactly 1/4" from each corner. Press seam allowances open after sewing each seam.*

1. Referring to Cube Assembly Diagram, sew squares together. Sew A, B, C, and D together. Sew E to the top edge and F to the bottom edge of B.

2. Sew A and E, then A and F together. Sew E and C, then F and C together. Fold D over to make the block shape; pin. Leaving about 1 1/2" open for turning and stuffing, sew D to A, E, and F.

3. Turn pincushion right side out; press. Press seam allowances at opening 1/4" to inside.

4. Fill pincushion with your choice of filling. Whipstitch the opening closed.

5. Cut 4 4" lengths of rickrack. Trimming as needed, glue 1 length along each corner edge of pincushion.

6. Cut 2 17" lengths of rickrack. Trimming as needed, glue 1 length along seamline on bottom of pincushion. Repeat with remaining length along top of pincushion.

Cube Assembly Diagram

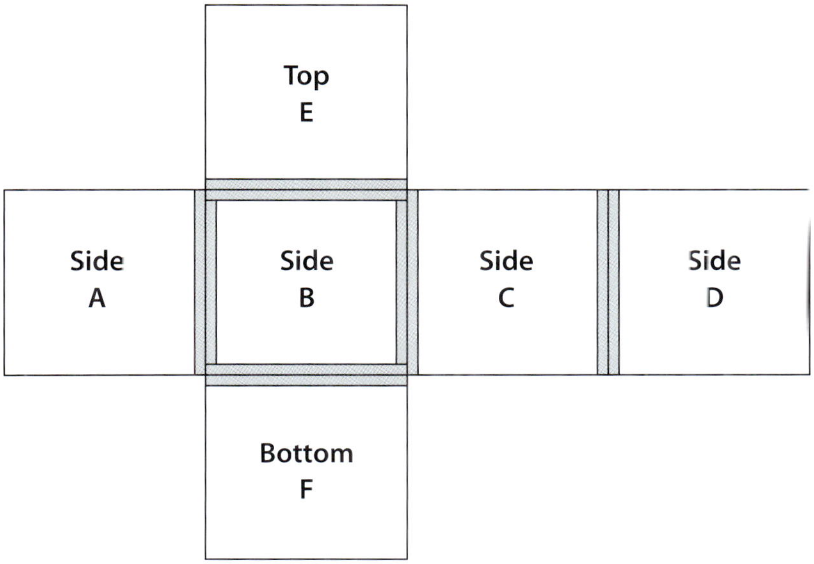

layered squares

SHOPPING LIST

- ☐ two $4^1/_2$" x $4^1/_2$" squares of red solid cotton fabric
- ☐ two 3" x 3" squares of orange solid cotton fabric
- ☐ two 2" x 2" squares of yellow solid cotton fabric
- ☐ red, orange, and yellow #3 pearl cotton
- ☐ all-purpose sewing thread
- ☐ embroidery needle
- ☐ filling of choice (see page 31)

Please read ***Basics****, page 31, before beginning project.*

To make the Pincushion

Note: *Match right sides and raw edges and use a 1/4" seam allowance throughout.*

1. Sew yellow squares together, leaving a small opening for turning. Trim seam allowances at corners. Turn squares right side out; press.

2. Repeat Step 1 with orange squares.

3. Using red pearl cotton and a Running Stitch, sew the yellow square to the orange square about 1/8" from edge.

4. To make pincushion top, pin stacked squares on right side of 1 red square.

5. Using yellow pearl cotton and a Running Stitch, sew the orange square to the red square about 1/8" from edge.

6. Using orange pearl cotton and a Running Stitch, sew 1/2" from each edge of each red square.

7. Sew top and remaining red square together, leaving about 1 1/2" open for turning. Trim seam allowances at corners.

8. Turn pincushion right side out; press. Press seam allowances at opening 1/4" to inside.

9. Fill pincushion with your choice of filling. Whipstitch the opening closed.

pocket

SHOPPING LIST

- ☐ $3^1/_2$" x 4" rectangle of navy solid cotton fabric
- ☐ $2^1/_2$" x 4" rectangle of orange print cotton fabric
- ☐ two 4" x 5" rectangles of orange polka dot print cotton fabric
- ☐ all-purpose sewing thread
- ☐ 14" length of $^3/_8$" wide navy grosgrain ribbon
- ☐ $^3/_4$" diameter button
- ☐ filling of choice (see page 31)

*Please read **Basics**, page 31, before beginning project.*

To make the Pincushion

***Note:** Match right sides and raw edges and use a $^1/_4$" seam allowance throughout.*

1. Press 1 long edge of orange print rectangle $^3/_8$" to wrong side. Topstitch along folded edge.
2. Repeat Step 1 with the navy rectangle.
3. With right sides facing up and matching raw edges, layer 1 orange polka dot rectangle, navy rectangle, and orange print rectangle. Baste layers together along side and bottom edges.
4. Matching raw edges, place remaining orange polka dot rectangle on top of stacked rectangles. Sew pieces together, leaving about $1^1/_2$" open along top edge for turning. Trim seam allowances at corners.
5. Turn pincushion right side out; press. Press seam allowances at opening $^1/_4$" to inside.

6. Fill pincushion with your choice of filling. Whipstitch the opening closed.
7. Tie ribbon in a bow; hand sew to top of lower pocket.

rickrack

SHOPPING LIST

- ☐ $4^1/_2$" x $4^1/_2$" square of pink striped cotton fabric
- ☐ $4^1/_2$" x $4^1/_2$" square and $4^1/_2$" x $2^3/_4$" rectangle of gold print cotton fabric
- ☐ $4^1/_2$" length of gold rickrack
- ☐ all-purpose sewing thread
- ☐ 3 gold buttons - $^5/_8$" diameter
- ☐ filling of choice (see page 31)

*Please read **Basics**, page 31, before beginning project.*

To make the Pincushion

***Note:** Match right sides and raw edges and use a $^1/_4$" seam allowance unless otherwise indicated.*

1. Press 1 long edge of gold rectangle $^1/_4$" to wrong side; press $^1/_4$" to wrong side again. Place rickrack along folded edge; topstitch in place.
2. Sew buttons to rectangle above rickrack. (Be sure outer buttons are at least $^1/_2$" from edge.)
3. To make pincushion top, match raw edges and baste wrong side of rectangle on right side of striped square.
4. Sew gold square and pincushion top together, leaving about $1^1/_2$" open for turning. Trim seam allowances at corners.
5. Turn pincushion right side out; press. Press seam allowances at opening $^1/_4$" to inside.
6. Fill pincushion with your choice of filling. Whipstitch the opening closed.

stacked

SHOPPING LIST

- ☐ two 4$^{1}/_{2}$" x 4$^{1}/_{2}$" squares of navy print cotton fabric
- ☐ two 3$^{1}/_{2}$" x 3$^{1}/_{2}$" squares of teal print cotton fabric
- ☐ two 2$^{1}/_{2}$" x 2$^{1}/_{2}$" squares of orange print cotton fabric
- ☐ $^{5}/_{8}$ yard of $^{3}/_{8}$" wide grosgrain ribbon
- ☐ grosgrain ribbon rosette to match ribbon **or** $^{3}/_{8}$ yard of $^{3}/_{8}$" wide grosgrain ribbon (for making your own rosette)
- ☐ all-purpose sewing thread
- ☐ long embroidery needle
- ☐ emery sand or crushed walnut shells for navy pincushion
- ☐ filling of choice (see page 31) for teal and orange pincushions

*Please read **Basics**, page 31, before beginning project.*

To make the Pincushion

***Note:** Match right sides and raw edges and use a 1/4" seam allowance throughout.*

1. Sew navy squares together, leaving about 1 1/2" open for turning. Trim seam allowances at corners.

2. Turn pincushion right side out; press. Press seam allowances at opening 1/4" to inside.

3. Fill pincushion with emery sand or crushed walnut shells. Whipstitch the opening closed.

4. Repeat Steps 1-3 with teal squares and then orange squares, filling pincushion with desired filling.

5. Stack pincushions from largest to smallest. With doubled strand of thread, insert needle from top to bottom through center of all pincushions and pull thread through. Insert needle from bottom to top through center of all pincushions and pull thread through. Do not tie off thread.

6. Cut two 10" lengths of ribbon. Insert needle through ends of both ribbons and take a small stitch to tack ends in place **(Fig. 1)**. Bring other ends of ribbons around pincushions to top and tack in place. Trim ribbon ends as needed. Sew rosette on center top.

To make your own rosette:
Cut a 12" length of ribbon. Thread hand sewing needle with doubled strand of thread. Make Running Stitches 1/8" to 1/4" apart along center of ribbon. Gently tug ends of thread to gather ribbon. Bring ends of ribbon together to form a circle, then take a few stitches along bottom edges of ribbon to gather into a rosette shape.

Fig. 1

pleated

SHOPPING LIST

- ☐ 6" x 9" rectangle of navy flower print cotton fabric
- ☐ 7" x 7" square of turquoise striped print cotton fabric
- ☐ 6" x 6" square of turquoise print cotton fabric
- ☐ all-purpose sewing thread
- ☐ 3/4" diameter button
- ☐ filling of choice (see page 31)

*Please read **Basics**, page 31, before beginning project.*

To make the Pincushion

***Note:** Match right sides and raw edges and use a $^1/_4$" seam allowance throughout.*

1. From navy flower print fabric, cut 3 small rectangles $1^1/_2$" x $3^1/_2$" and 2 large rectangles 2" x $5^1/_2$".

2. From turquoise striped print fabric, cut 2 small rectangles $1^1/_2$" x $3^1/_2$" and 2 large rectangles $1^1/_2$" x $5^1/_2$".

3. From turquoise print fabric, cut 2 small rectangles $1^1/_2$" x $3^1/_2$" and 1 large rectangle $2^1/_2$" x $5^1/_2$".

4. To make pincushion front, alternate fabrics and sew long edges of navy flower print small rectangles and turquoise print small rectangles together. Press seam allowances toward navy flower print fabrics.

5. On right side, bring seamlines of 2 adjacent navy flower print rectangles together, forming a pleat in 1 turquoise print rectangle; pin and press. Baste across ends of pleat. Repeat for another pleat in remaining turquoise print rectangle (**Fig. 1**).

6. Sew 1 turquoise striped print small rectangle to 1 end of pleats; press rectangle and seam allowances away from pleats. Repeat for opposite end of pleats.

7. Sew 1 turquoise striped print large rectangle to side of pincushion; press rectangle and seam allowances away from pleats. Repeat for opposite side of pincushion.

8. To make pincushion back, alternate fabrics and sew long edges of remaining large rectangles together. Press seam allowances toward navy flower print fabric.

9. Sew pincushion front to pincushion back, leaving about $1^1/_2$" open for turning. Trim seam allowances at corners.

10. Turn pincushion right side out; press. Press seam allowances at opening $^1/_4$" to inside.

11. Fill pincushion with your choice of filling. Whipstitch the opening closed.

Fig. 1

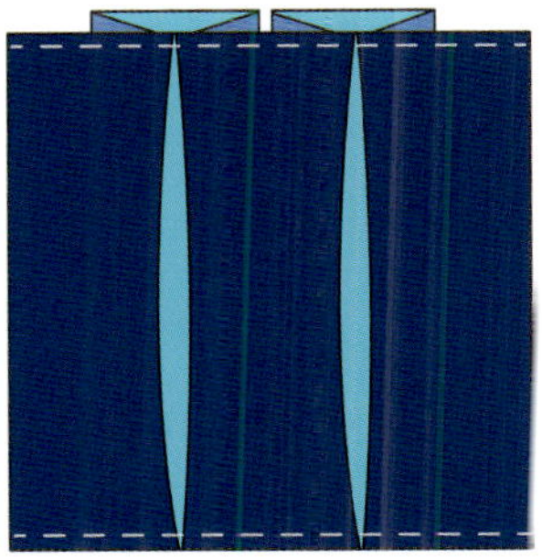

hexagon

SHOPPING LIST

- ☐ 2 1/2" x 15" rectangle of green batik cotton fabric
- ☐ 2 1/2" x 15" rectangle of turquoise batik cotton fabric
- ☐ 2 1/2" x 15" rectangle of purple batik cotton fabric
- ☐ all-purpose sewing thread
- ☐ 1 1/4" diameter decorative button
- ☐ tracing paper
- ☐ filling of choice (see page 31)

*Please read **Basics**, page 31, before beginning project.*

To make the Pincushion

***Note:** Match right sides and raw edges and use a 1/4" seam allowance throughout. Begin and end stitching lines at each dot. Trim seam allowances above dot. Press seam allowances open after sewing each seam.*

1. Trace pattern onto tracing paper. Using pattern, cut two hexagon sections from each fabric.

2. Referring to **Hexagon Assembly Diagram**, sew 1 top pointed end of each hexagon section to adjacent hexagon section from top dot to side edge dot to form a star shape.

3. Sew side seams from dot to dot.

4. Sew from side seam dot to bottom dot, leaving a small opening in 1 seam for turning.

5. Turn pincushion right side out; press. Press seam allowances at opening 1/4" to inside. Sew decorative button to center top.

6. Fill pincushion with your choice of filling. Whipstitch the opening closed.

Hexagon Assembly Diagram

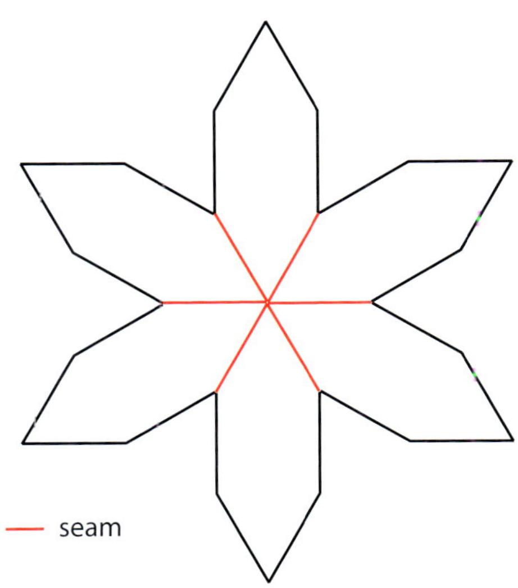

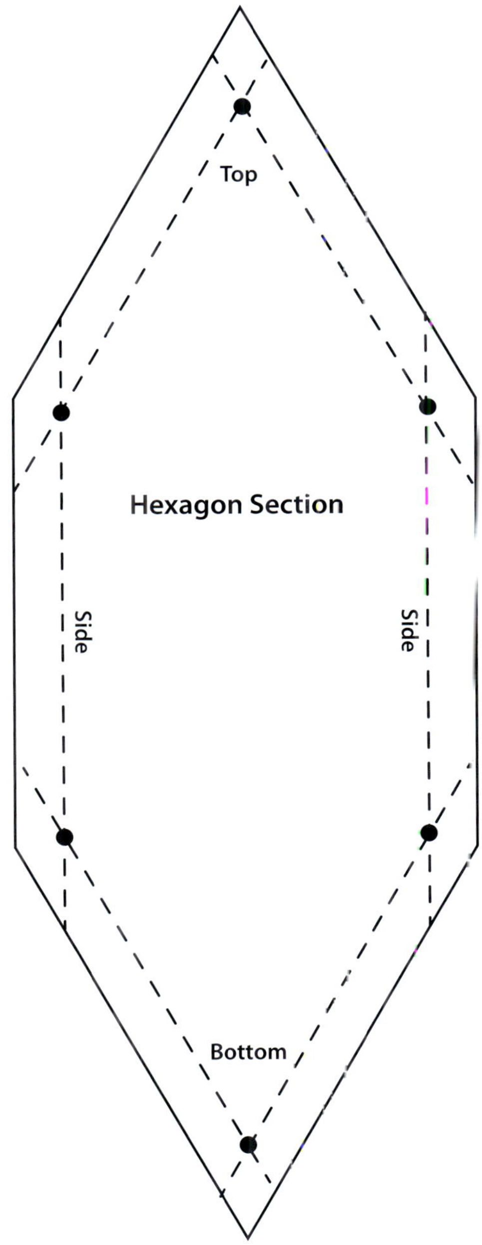

sewing machine

SHOPPING LIST

- ☐ 2$^1/_2$" x 18" strip of purple batik cotton fabric
- ☐ 2$^1/_2$" x 18" strip of orange batik cotton fabric
- ☐ 2$^1/_2$" x 18" strip of multi-color batik cotton fabric
- ☐ 5" x 6" piece of lightweight fusible interfacing
- ☐ size #3 pearl cotton
- ☐ all-purpose sewing thread
- ☐ embroidery needle
- ☐ polyester fiberfill

*Please read **Basics**, page 31, before beginning project.*

To make the Pincushion

Note: *Match right sides and raw edges and use a 1/4" seam allowance throughout.*

1. Sew long edges of strips together.
2. Refer to **Fig. 1** and follow manufacturer's instructions to fuse interfacing on wrong side of fabric 1/2" from 1 short edge and 1/4" from side edges.
3. Press short edges 3/8" to wrong side. Matching pressed edges, fold piece in half. Sew long edges together; trim corners at fold.
4. Turn pincushion right side out; press.
5. Using pearl cotton, stitch a Running Stitch about 1/4" from edge along the 2 sewn edges.
6. Fill bottom 3" of pincushion with fiberfill; be sure to stuff corners. Using pearl cotton, stitch a Running Stitch parallel to and about 3" from folded end of pincushion. Using pearl cotton and a Running Stitch, sew open end closed about 1/4" from edge.

Fig. 1

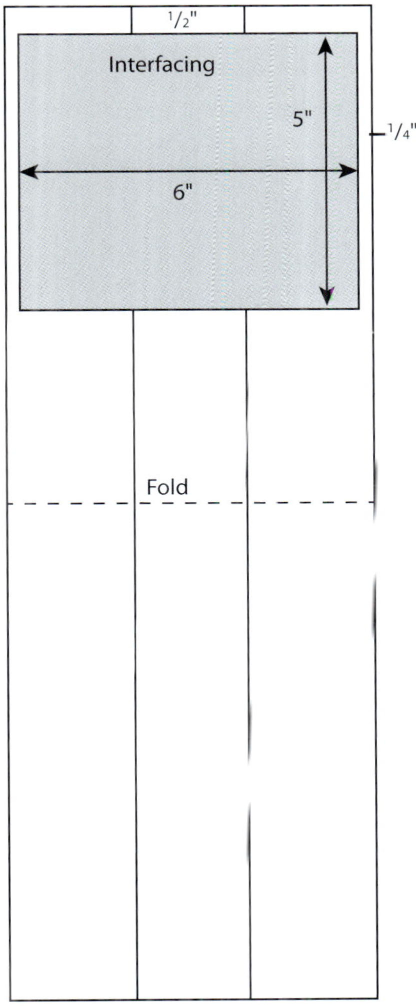

prairie points

SHOPPING LIST

- ☐ 5" x 16" strip of turquoise print cotton fabric
- ☐ 5½" x 11" rectangle of floral print cotton fabric
- ☐ 7" x 10" rectangle of pink print cotton fabric
- ☐ all-purpose sewing thread
- ☐ polyester fiberfill
- ☐ tracing paper
- ☐ filling of choice (see page 31)

*Please read **Basics**, page 31, before beginning project.*

To make the Pincushion

***Note:** Match right sides and raw edges and use a 1/4" seam allowance throughout.*

1. From turquoise print fabric, cut pincushion sides 1 1/2" x 14 1/2" and 6 small squares 2 1/2" x 2 1/2".

2. Trace hexagon patterns (page 32) onto tracing paper. From floral print fabric, use patterns to cut 1 large hexagon and 1 small hexagon.

3. From pink print fabric, cut 6 large squares 3" x 3".

4. To make a large prairie point, match wrong sides and fold 1 large square in half; press (**Fig. 1**). Fold each upper corner down to meet at center bottom edge to form a triangle; press (**Fig. 2**). This is the right side of the prairie point. Make a total of 6 large prairie points.

5. Repeat Step 4 using the small squares to make 6 small prairie points.

6. Matching right sides and beginning and ending at a dot, sew 1 small prairie point to each edge of the small hexagon. Press the seam allowances toward the wrong side of the hexagon.

7. Matching right sides and beginning and ending at a dot, sew the large prairie points to each edge of the large hexagon.

8. To make pincushion top, align the small prairie points with the points on the large hexagon and center the small hexagon, right side up, on the right side of the large hexagon; pin. Topstitch in the seam line around 5 sides of the small hexagon. Before stitching the final side, stuff the small hexagon with fiberfill. Topstitch along the final side.

9. Sew short ends of pincushion sides together to form a loop; press the seam allowances open. Flatten the sides. Fold sides into thirds. Make small clips (slightly less than 1/4") along top and bottom of sides at each fold to divide pincushion sides into 6 sections.

10. Taking care not to catch prairie points in stitching, match hexagon points on pincushion top to clips on sides and sew pincushion top to pincushion sides.

11. Leaving 1 side open for turning, repeat Step 10 to sew remaining large hexagon to pincushion sides.

12. Turn pincushion right side out; press. Press seam allowances at opening 1/4" to inside.

13. Fill pincushion with your choice of filling. Whipstitch the opening closed.

Fig. 1

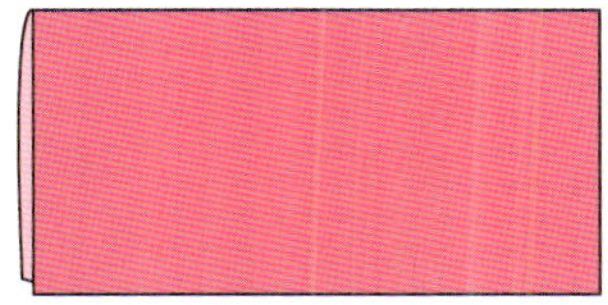

Fig. 2

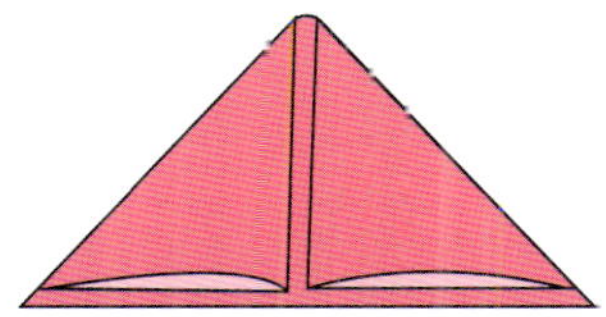

trio

SHOPPING LIST

- ☐ two $4\frac{1}{2}$" x $4\frac{1}{2}$" squares of pink print cotton fabric
- ☐ two $4\frac{1}{2}$" x $4\frac{1}{2}$" squares of green print cotton fabric
- ☐ two $4\frac{1}{2}$" x $4\frac{1}{2}$" squares of blue print cotton fabric
- ☐ all-purpose sewing thread
- ☐ $1\frac{3}{8}$ yards of $\frac{7}{8}$" wide grosgrain ribbon
- ☐ $\frac{1}{2}$ yard of mini ball fringe
- ☐ fabric glue
- ☐ filling of choice (see page 31)

*Please read **Basics**, page 31, before beginning project.*

To make the Pincushion

***Note:** Match right sides and raw edges and use a $\frac{1}{4}$" seam allowance throughout.*

1. Cut ten $4\frac{1}{2}$" lengths of ribbon; set aside.

For pink pincushion:

2. With right sides facing up, pin 1 ribbon length parallel to and 1" from 1 edge of top square. Pin second ribbon perpendicular to first ribbon and 1" from edge of square. Baste $\frac{1}{8}$" from each ribbon end.
3. Sew top and bottom together, leaving about $1\frac{1}{2}$" open for turning. Trim seam allowances at corners.
4. Turn pincushion right side out; press. Press seam allowances at opening $\frac{1}{4}$" to inside.
5. Fill pincushion with your choice of filling. Whipstitch the opening closed.
6. Glue fringe around edges of pincushion.

Fig. 1

Fig. 2

Fig. 3

Fig. 4

For green pincushion:

7. With right sides facing up, pin 1 ribbon length parallel to and 1" from 1 edge of top square. Pin second ribbon parallel to first ribbon and 1 1/4" from opposite edge of square **(Fig. 1)**. Baste 1/8" from each ribbon end.

8. Weave second pair of ribbons under and over first pair. Pin 1 ribbon length parallel to and 1" from 1 edge of top square. Pin second ribbon parallel to first ribbon and 1 1/4" from opposite edge of square **(Fig. 2)**. Baste 1/8" from each ribbon end.

9. Repeat Steps 3-6 to complete green pincushion.

For blue pincushion:

10. With right sides facing up, pin 1 ribbon parallel to and 3/4" from 1 edge of top square. Pin second ribbon parallel to first ribbon and 3/4" from opposite edge of square **(Fig. 3)**. Baste 1/8" from each ribbon end.

11. Weave second pair of ribbons under and over first pair. Pin 1 ribbon parallel to and 3/4" from 1 edge of top square. Pin second ribbon parallel to first ribbon and 3/4" from opposite edge of square **(Fig. 4)**. Baste 1/8" from each ribbon end.

12. Repeat Steps 3-6 to complete blue pincushion.

basics

To make assembling your pincushion easier and more enjoyable, we encourage you to carefully read all of the **Basics**, study the color photographs, and familiarize yourself with the individual project instructions before beginning.

GENERAL SUPPLIES

Filling

If you desire a weighted pincushion that will stay in place when you're using it you will want to fill it with emery sand or crushed walnut shells.

Emery sand is an excellent product for filling your pincushion and it helps keep pins and needles sharp. You can find it at larger hardware stores where it's sold with supplies for sand blasting. There are also sources online that sell small quantities just for filling pincushions.

Crushed walnut shells are another good product to use for filling your pincushion. They are sold at pet stores for bedding. This material is a bit more coarse than emery sand yet adds a nice weighted feel. This ***would not*** be a good choice for someone who is allergic to nuts.

Thread

To construct the pincushion, you will need all-purpose sewing thread. Be sure to use the same color in the bobbin and the needle. Match the thread color to the fabric color or choose a contrasting color.

Pearl cotton

Some pincushions require pearl cotton. Do not separate the pearl cotton; use it as it comes off the skein or ball. Match the pearl cotton color to the fabric or choose a contrasting color.

Glue

Use small drops of fabric glue to glue the trims to the pincushion.

Scissors or rotary cutter, cutting mat, and quilting ruler

When cutting fabric, very sharp scissors or a rotary cutter are excellent choices. Fabric can be quickly and accurately cut with rotary cutting equipment but scissors are easier to use when cutting curved pieces.

Sewing Machine

A sewing machine is needed for making the pincushion. Begin with a new needle (size 70 or 80). Set the machine stitch length to either 2.5 or 3 (11 or 9 stitches per inch, respectively). Clean the bobbin casing regularly as you sew to remove the lint that might accumulate there.

HAND STITCHES

Running Stitch

"Stab" the needle straight up and down through the fabric to work the neatest stitches. Come up at 1, go down at 2, and come up at 3 (**Fig. 1**). Continue working in the same manner, trying to make the stitches the same length and the same distance apart.

Fig. 1

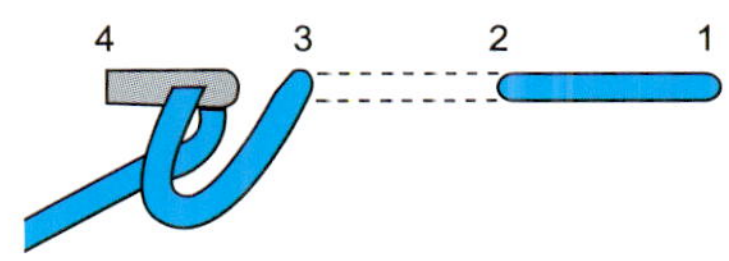

Whipstitch

Come up at 1. Go down at 2, directly across from 1 (**Fig. 2**). Come up at 3, approximately $^{1}/_{16}$" away from 1. Continue working in the same manner.

Fig. 2

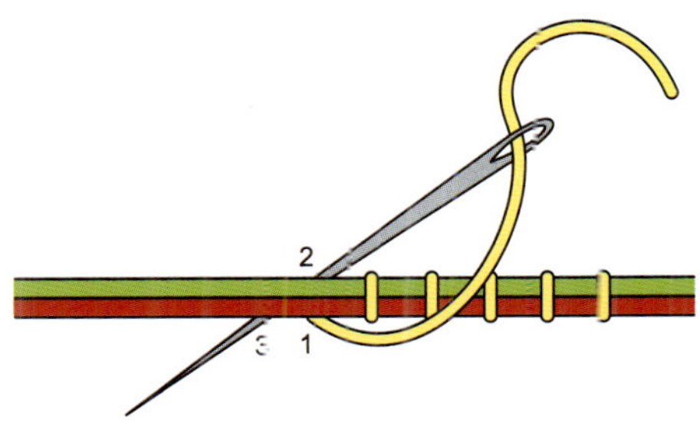

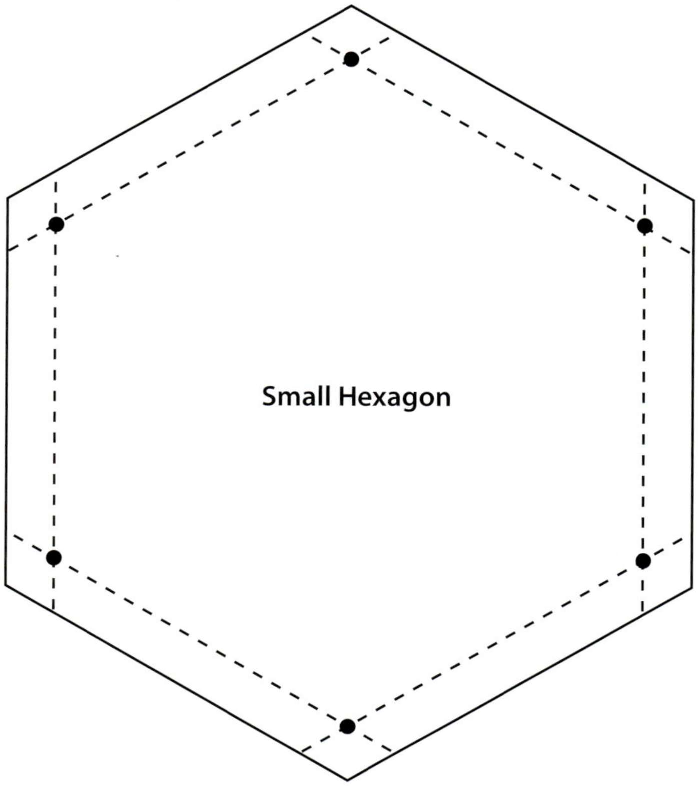

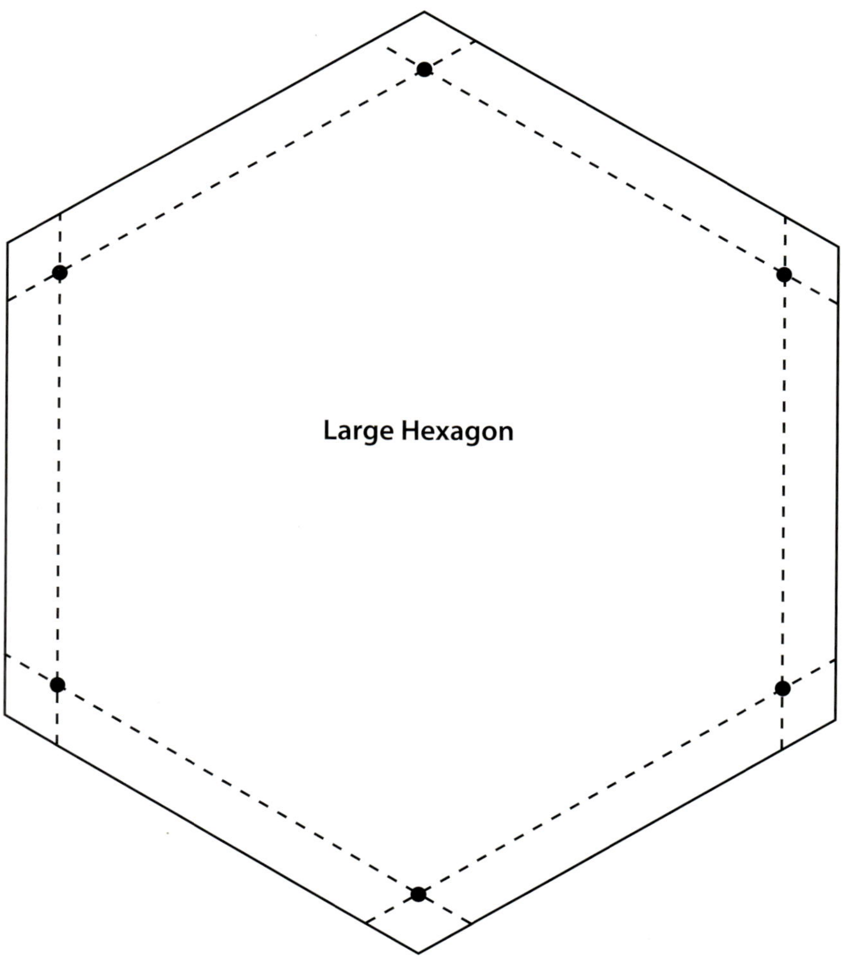

Edie Eckman

Edie Eckman sewed her first dress at age 8, a Gunne Sax-inspired prom dress in high school, and countless clothes, curtains and home dec projects in the ensuing years. A well-known professional knit and crochet designer and teacher for the past two decades, she is now turning her design talents to sewing. Pincushions to Sew is her first sewing book, but it won't be her last. Find her at www.edieeckman.com.

Production Team: Technical Editor – Lisa Lancaster; Technical Associate – Mary Sullivan Hutcheson; Editorial Writer - Susan Frantz Wiles; Senior Graphic Artist – Lora Puls; Graphic Artist - Kellie McAnulty; Photostylists – Lori Wenger and Lora Puls; Photographers - Jason Masters and Stephanie Johnson.

We have made every effort to ensure that these instructions are accurate and complete. We cannot, however, be responsible for human error, typographical mistakes, or variations in individual work.